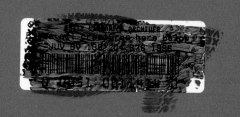

# BLESS ALL CREATURES HERE BELOW

A Celebration for the Blessing of the Animals

Time:

Place:

**Morehouse Publishing**

*Editorial Office:*
871 Ethan Allen Highway
Suite 204
Ridgefield, CT  06877

*Corporate Office:*
P.O. Box 1321
Harrisburg, PA  17105

11/97

**Library of Congress Cataloging-in-Publication Data**
Brown, Judith Gwyn.
  Bless all creatures here below : a celebration for the blessing of
the animals / written and illustrated by Judith Gwyn Brown : music
by Herbert G. Draesel, Jr.
    p.   cm.
    ISBN 0-8192-1665-8  (hc)
    1. Hymns, American.   2. Children's liturgies.   3. Animals–
–Religious aspects—Christianity.   4. Benediction.   I. Draesel,
Herbert G.   II. Title.
  BV199.C4B76   1996                                  96-23109
  274'.2—dc20                                            CIP

$15.95

Permission is granted for use of the half-title page as the basis of a poster ready for adding details for a local event. Enlarge on a photocopier to the desired size, adding time, place, and other particulars as needed.

*Printed in Malaysia*

10  9  8  7  6  5  4  3  2  1

This book is dedicated to the people
of the Church of the Holy Trinity, N.Y.C.,
who open their arms to all of God's creatures,
and welcome them Sunday by Sunday
as they meet for divine worship.

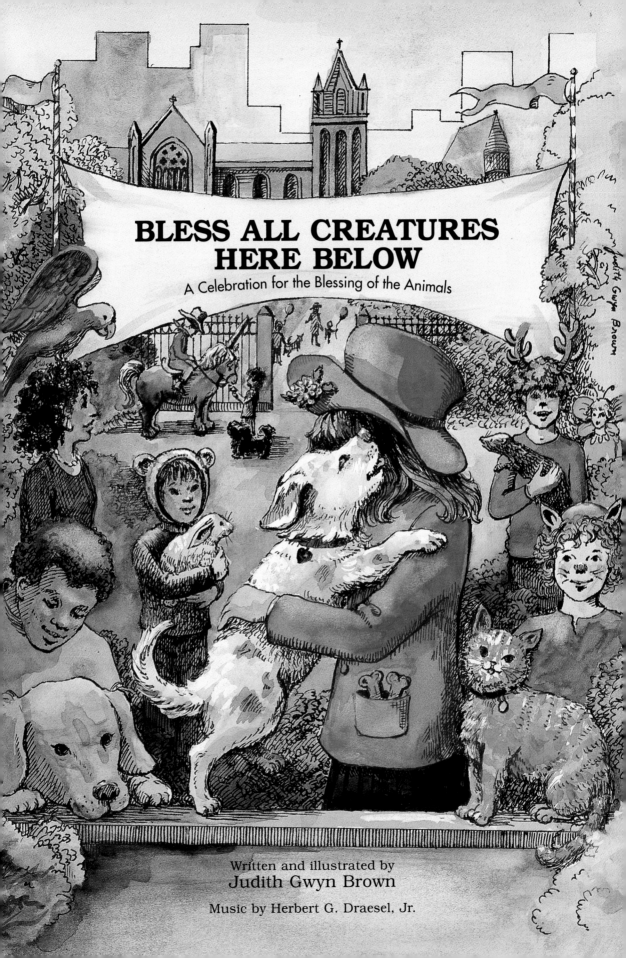

# BLESS ALL CREATURES HERE BELOW

A Celebration for the Blessing of the Animals

Written and illustrated by
Judith Gwyn Brown

Music by Herbert G. Draesel, Jr.

oday we celebrate a feast,
A holiday for man and beast.
We think of every friend
  who speaks
In barks and purrs and roars
  and squeaks.
As we sing, we keep in mind
Beings of a different kind.

Bless all creatures here below,
Lord, from whom all blessings flow.

We think of squirrels in the park
At play from morning light 'til dark,

And birds that sing on leafy boughs

In green fields with sheep and cows;

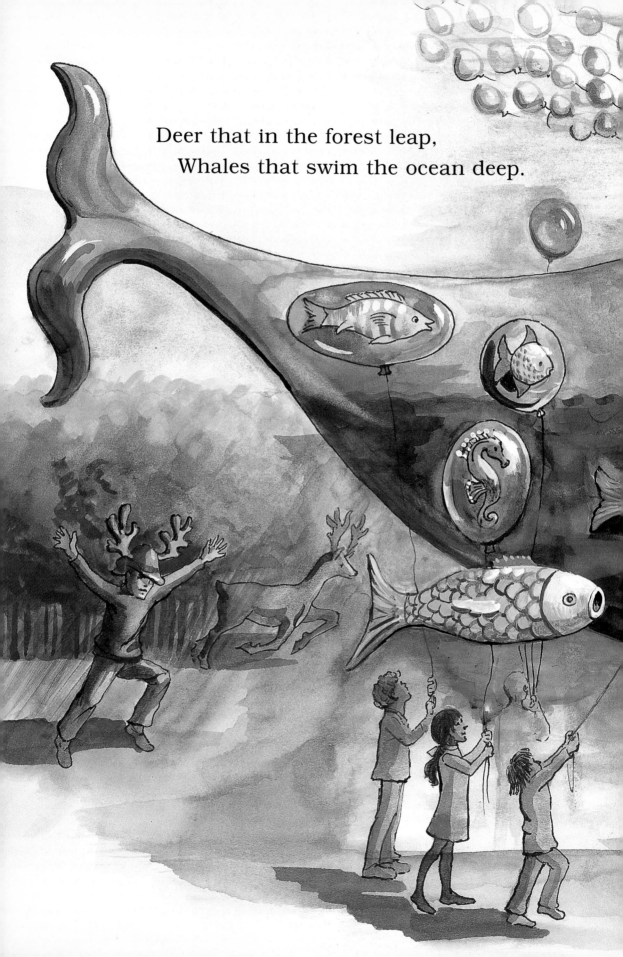

Deer that in the forest leap,
Whales that swim the ocean deep.

Together with our pets we meet
New friends with whiskers, tails that greet.
Muzzles wet beside our cheek
Show us love they cannot speak.
Hold them tight so they will know
Where we are, they too will go.

The Unicorn

Behold in pictures and in books

the unicorn with gentle looks;

Dragons snort a fiery blaze,

Monkeys act out human ways.
In these stories we can see
Beasts resembling you and me.

God made the tortoise
in its shell,
And bugs and butterflies
as well.

In Noah's ark beasts walked as two,
Safe from stormy winds that blew;

And some knelt on Christmas morn
In the shed where Christ was born.

Lord, here beside our friends we stand,
Their earthly care within our hand.
Watching those we hold so dear,
We can feel your presence near.
When we come at last to you,
Let our creatures be there too.

Bless all creatures here below,
Lord, from whom all blessings flow.

# BLESS ALL CREATURES HERE BELOW

1. To - day we cel - e - brate a feast, a hol - i - day for man and beast. We think of ev - ery friend who speaks, barks and purrs and roars and squeaks.

2. We think of squir - rels in the park at play from morn - ing light 'til dark, and birds that sing on leaf - y boughs in green fields with sheep and cows;

3. To - ge - ther with our pets we meet new friends with whis - kers, tails that greet. Muz - zles wet be - side our cheek show us love they can - not speak.

4. Be - hold in pic - tures and in books the u - ni - corn with gen - tle looks; dra - gons snort a fi - ery blaze, mon - keys act out hu - man ways.

5. God made the tor - toise in its shell, and bugs and but - ter - flies as well. In No - ah's ark beasts walked as two, safe from stor - my winds that blew;

6. Lord, here be - side our friends we stand, their earth - ly care with - in our hand. Watch - ing those we hold so dear, we can feel your pres - ence near.

1. As we sing, we keep in mind be - ings of a
2. Deer that in the for - est leap, whales that swim the
3. Hold them tight so they will know where we are, they
4. In these stor - ies we can see beasts re - sem - bling
5. And some knelt on Christ - mas morn in the shed where
6. When we come at last to you, let our crea - tures

1. dif - ferent kind.
2. o - cean deep.
3. too will go.
4. you and me.
5. Christ was born.
6. be there too.

Bless all crea - tures

here be - low, Lord, from whom all bless - ings flow.

*Words by Judith Gwyn Brown*
*Tune: Yorkville*
*Music by Herbert G. Draesel, Jr.*

# A SERVICE FOR THE BLESSING OF ANIMALS

*Leader:*     The Lord has created every living creature and delights in all that he has made.

*Response:*  O come let us adore him.

Hymn:       *Bless All Creatures Here Below*, vs. 1-5


## A Reading from the Book of Genesis

Then God said to Noah and to his sons with him, "As for me, I am establishing my covenant with you and your descendants after you, and with every living creature that is with you, the birds, the domestic animals, and every animal of the earth with you, as many as came out of the ark. When I bring clouds over the earth and the bow is seen in the clouds, I will remember my covenant that is between me and you and every living creature of all flesh; and the waters shall never again become a flood to destroy all flesh. When the bow is in the clouds, I will see it and remember the everlasting covenant between God and every living creature of all flesh that is on the earth." God said to Noah, "This is the sign of the covenant that I have established between me and all flesh that is on the earth" (Gen. 9:8-10, 14-17).

The suggested Psalm is Psalm 104: 25-37.


## A Song of Creation

O Let the Earth bless the Lord: Yea, let it praise him and
     magnify him forever.
O ye Mountains and Hills, bless ye the Lord: praise him, and
     magnify him forever.

O ye Wells, bless ye the Lord: praise him, and magnify him forever.

O ye seas and floods, bless ye the Lord: praise him, and magnify him forever.

O ye Whales, and all that move in the waters, bless ye the Lord: praise him, and magnify him forever.

O all ye Fowls of the air, bless ye the Lord: praise him, and magnify him forever.

O all ye Beasts and Cattle, bless ye the Lord: praise him and magnify him forever.

O ye Children of Men, bless ye the Lord: praise him and magnify him forever.

**Prayer**

O Lord, who has looked upon all of his creation and declared that it was good, we thank you for the animals, with whom we share this earth, and particularly for those which you have given into our care. We pray that you will guard them and tend to their necessities, relieve their suffering, protect them from exploitation, and let each of us see in them the beauty and glory of your creative hand. As you raised your servant Francis to declare oneness of all your work, give us gentle spirits, and help us to be instruments of your loving providence, that we all may abound in your glory. *Amen.*

**As each animal is blessed:**

*Leader*: May God's blessing be upon you (N) and may you flourish in the care and joy of those whose lives you share.

*Leader*: The peace of the Lord be always with you.

*Response*: And also with you.

Hymn: *Bless All Creatures Here Below*, vs. 6

# BLESS ALL CREATURES HERE BELOW

Today we celebrate a feast,
A holiday for man and beast.
We think of every friend who speaks
In barks and purrs and roars and squeaks.
As we sing, we keep in mind
Beings of a different kind.

> *Refrain:*   Bless all creatures here below,
> Lord, from whom all blessings flow.

We think of squirrels in the park
At play from morning light 'til dark,
And birds that sing on leafy boughs
In green fields with sheep and cows;
Deer that in the forest leap,
Whales that swim the ocean deep.
> *Refrain*

Together with our pets we meet
New friends with whiskers, tails that greet.
Muzzles wet beside our cheek
Show us love they cannot speak.
Hold them tight so they will know
Where we are, they too will go.
> *Refrain*

Behold in pictures and in books
The unicorn with gentle looks;
Dragons snort a fiery blaze,
Monkeys act out human ways.
In these stories we can see
Beasts resembling you and me.
> *Refrain*

God made the tortoise in its shell,
And bugs and butterflies as well.
In Noah's ark beasts walked as two,
Safe from stormy winds that blew;
And some knelt on Christmas morn
In the shed where Christ was born.
> *Refrain*

Lord, here beside our friends we stand,
Their earthly care within our hand.
Watching those we hold so dear,
We can feel your presence near.
When we come at last to you,
Let our creatures be there too.
> *Refrain*